If a man does not care about his clothes
they hang on him like old clothes on a
scarecrow in the cornfield.

ETIQUETTE
FOR THE
WELL-DRESSED
MAN

Compiled by
Jan Barnes

Copper Beech Publishing

Published in Great Britain by
Copper Beech Publishing Ltd
© Copper Beech Publishing Ltd 1998

ISBN 1 898617 16 3

A CIP catalogue record for this book is available from the
British Library.

Copper Beech Publishing Ltd
P O Box 159 East Grinstead
Sussex England RH19 4FS

Why do some men look smart and others dowdy?

INTRODUCTION

'Only millionaires and tramps can afford to dress badly.'

To become a millionaire - or at least to get on in life - a man needs to be well-dressed. Dress well and you increase your self-confidence and self-respect.

When you meet a stranger, whether socially or in business, he or she judges you firstly according to your choice of clothing.

It need not cost any more to dress well than to dress badly; indeed, the well-dressed man is more economical than a slovenly man.

A man has no business to make an eyesore of himself by dressing badly. When you put on the wrong clothes, your error of taste is almost as great as the man who uses his knife to eat instead of his fork!

Consider the following hints taken from late Victorian and Edwardian writers with regard to the art of being well-dressed.

The advice is fun to read and useful to any man wishing to succeed in life - or perhaps become a millionaire!

WHY DO SOME MEN LOOK SMART AND OTHERS DOWDY?

The well-dressed man takes care of his clothes and so gets full value out of them. The slovenly man wears the same suit day after day and hacks it out in a couple of months.

The well-dressed man buys more clothes in the first instance, and by wearing each suit alternately makes a suit last longer than two months.

The man who is well dressed has his things kept in the right order, and that means a saving of time and temper! Also, the habit of keeping clothes in order extends to other matters. A well-dressed man always has a well-ordered house.

It is a mistake to suppose that it is a waste of time to dress well; a well-dressed man need not spend any more time in dressing than a badly dressed man does.

WHY DO SOME MEN LOOK SMART AND OTHERS DOWDY?

If you are engaged in any business or profession, you are much more likely to succeed if you are well-dressed than if you are badly dressed.

If you are married, one of your duties to your wife is to be well dressed. No woman with any self respect likes a slovenly man. If you are not married, you owe it to your future wife.

A well-dressed man wears clothes that suit him, clothes that are recognised as being the proper clothes for the occasion. He doesn't go down the river in a straw hat, black morning coat and flannel trousers!

WHEN YOU VISIT YOUR TAILOR

Never mind if you have got an inch bigger ...

When you visit your tailor, be your normal self. Do not hold your breath when the tape is going round what is left of your shapely waist.

An experienced tailor knows what you are up to. He has already cast a professional eye over your manly form; he knows that you cannot keep up the strain for more than a minute or two and that your beautiful crescent-shaped waist will reassert itself while he is measuring you for trousers.

Vow that you will not eat potatoes and bread in the future and that you walk for at least two hours every day, but do not compress your waist.

Never mind if you have got an inch bigger in the waist. Very likely it isn't your fault and you can comfort yourself with the reflection that many a man of the lean kind would welcome that extra inch.

✎ A Useful Hint ✎

Do not allow your tailor to blunder with regard to a ticket pocket. If this is made absurdly small, so that you have great difficulty in putting your fingers into it, it will stretch out of shape and 'sag' away from the rest of the coat.

COATS AND WAISTCOATS

The best is the cheapest in the long run.

Dust and fluff are less likely to be harboured by a hard worsted material with a perfectly smooth surface. This wears – to use a tailor's expression – 'cleaner'.

The frock coat must be either black or grey. There are, of course, many different qualities of black worsted and the best is by far the cheapest in the long run.

The frock coat fits well into the figure. The sleeves are narrow; there is no spare material in the skirts and the coat does not reach lower than the knees. The coat is bound with braid, is cut high at the neck and is generally worn buttoned up.

When ordering a coat from his tailor a man should state whether he is going to keep his coat buttoned up or unbuttoned.

*If a man has any defects in his figure
the frock coat will hide them.*

❧ *A Useful Hint* ❧

When you're putting on a new coat, get your
shoulders well into the shoulders of the coat. Pull
the coat well over them; put your arms inside the
coat for this purpose much in the same careful
way that you assist your wife to put her puffy
dress sleeves into the shoulders of her jacket.

Then, button the coat up.

Never mind if the thermometer is ninety in
the shade and you feel that you would rather not
wear any clothes at all. Button the coat up, and
keep it buttoned up!

Go about with it like that. You don't get
something for nothing in this world, not even the
reputation of being well-dressed!

You must wear your coat buttoned up for the
first six times at least. After that it ought to be
moulded to your figure.

*A very smart outfit to go racing in is
a light grey worsted frock coat suit.*

If you are wearing a black frock or morning coat you will wear striped trousers of some quiet pattern. There is one exception to this rule. In the summer time, if you are middle-aged, you may wear black and white check trousers.

If you wear a morning coat your trousers will show more and must therefore be absolutely blameless.

The word 'morning' does not mean at all that it may be worn only in the mornings. A smart morning coat may be worn by a young man on almost every occasion in town. It can be worn to a wedding – or to a garden party in the afternoon!

HOW TO RUIN A GOOD COAT

... take it off, drop it on a chair and sit on it

Go for the pockets if you want to ruin your coat. If they are small, fill them up; weigh them down with heavy pocket-books and in a short space of time you will succeed in stretching your coat out of all shape.

When you take it off, drop your coat on a chair and sit on it when you are undoing your boots. Leave the coat like that all night. You will be astonished to see how shabby the coat will look when you put it on again!

The other way of spoiling it is to hang it up by the narrow loop of ribbon that the tailor provides for the purpose. If you hang a coat for a day or two by the ribbon you will find that when you go to it again, the collar will have been dragged out of shape by the weight of the coat.

∞ *A Useful Hint* ∞

A well-made coat has a soft and easy finish.
There should be no unsightly 'puckers'. Clothes
that fit well wear twice as long.

OTHER COATS AND SUITS

People will think you are wearing a ready-made coat

The single breasted reefer coat is very popular. It is usually worn buttoned up but do not spoil it by bulging out the side pockets.

This coat should have no waist but remember this; if it is too long it will crease at the back every time you sit down. If it is too short you will have the satisfaction of knowing that people will think one of two things about you - that you are wearing the coat of your younger brother - or a ready-made coat!

There is no more useful suit than a navy blue serge suit. It is never out of fashion and you couldn't get a better all-round useful suit. You can pay up to 8 or 9 pounds for a suit, and the more you pay, the better value you get from it.

Flannel suiting was intended to be worn in the summer by men in town who had no particular reasons for wearing ordinary town clothes. These suits are much cooler than a tweed suit and if the suit is smartly cut, you can wear it at a garden party in the country.

❧ *A Useful Hint* ❧

Do not have country clothes very thick.
Even in winter you don't want very
thick clothes in the country because you
generally take far more exercise in the country
than you do in town and consequently you don't
feel the cold so much.

TROUSERS

A certain air of smartness ...

A **well-cut pair of trousers** must be comfortable to the man who is wearing them. Do not allow yourself to be persuaded by a tailor who tells you that 'they are sure to feel a little new' for the first time they are worn.

Trousers should not fit tightly nor should they be too loose at the seat.

Trousers should hang in straight lines from the hips and fork downwards. There should be no 'puckering' or surplus material about the fork. The seams should be made very neatly otherwise they will cockle all the way down the leg. The ends of the trousers should drop well over the boots in a small crease or two.

If when choosing a pair of trousers you find that the material stretches easily in your hands, discard it and go for another. It will be quite elastic enough when it is worn.

Some men think that they can add a certain air of smartness if they turn their trousers up. A gentleman should not turn his trousers up unless there is mud out of doors and he should take particular care to turn them down again before he enters a house.

If he is in any danger of forgetting, let him write it down on a piece of paper and pin it in his hat and say it over to himself when he is out on a muddy day.

When you turn your trousers up you collect a lot of mud and dirt and hostesses object to having mud brought into the house.

Keep your flannel trousers in a press when they are not being worn – that is in the summer time when you may want to wear them every day.

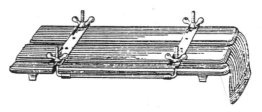

In the winter your flannel trousers should be put away, and if you want to keep the moth from them, take care that they are cleaned before being put away, and that they are absolutely dry.

There is nothing a moth likes more than a piece of damp flannel!

The trousers should be taken out of the drawer and shaken well at least once a fortnight.

✑ *A Useful Hint* ✑

A wise precaution is to pull the trousers up a
little before sitting down; this will save a great
deal of 'bagging' at the knees.

GETTING TROUSERS CREASED CORRECTLY

Mark your trousers with chalk ...

How can you be sure you are getting the trousers creased correctly?

Stand in front of a long glass with your trousers on and with your legs a few inches apart. Mark the trousers in the centre of the thigh, knee and near your feet with chalk. Then take the trousers off and fold them so that the chalk marks come in the front crease.

◈ *A Useful Hint* ◈

If you want a very sharp crease in your trousers, damp them before you put them in the press and then exert all the pressure you know.

PREVENT TROUSERS FROM GOING BAGGY AT THE KNEES

... have at least seven pairs ...

The gentleman who wishes to keep his **trousers in proper shape** must begin by having at least seven pairs. He should not be persuaded into wearing a pair of trousers more than once a week.

Any pair of trousers worn for three consecutive days will be out of shape at the end of the third day.

Great care must be taken of your trousers when they are not in use. The seams should be put together and then the trousers put into a trouser straightener or press. Trouser straighteners may cost half a crown apiece but they will last a lifetime.

If you have a pair of trousers that have gone at the knees, the best thing to do with them is to give them to the gardener. This is an unfailing remedy for all troubles connected with trousers!

SHIRTS

The very best quality plain white linen ...

The linen shirt is the cleanest looking and smartest but, if badly made, the most uncomfortable shirt that it is possible for a man to wear.

If the weather is cold, the man who wears a badly made white linen shirt will feel the cold more than if he wore a flannel shirt. If the weather is very hot, the same linen shirt will make a man feel uncomfortably hot.

But the fact remains that you can't beat the very best quality plain white linen shirts for all general purposes; in fact a man might lay in a stock of them and never wear any other kind of shirt, and he would not be absolutely wrong whatever he was doing.

If you are wearing a coloured shirt in town it should have white cuffs; if in the country, it may have cuffs of the same material as the shirt.

The soft-fronted shirt is usually made in a cotton material, but if a man is going to row hard, play tennis or take any hard exercise he should wear a soft-fronted shirt of fine flannel.

COLLARS AND TIES

No collar is perfect for long ...

The best collars are nearly perfect when they are in the shop, but when they have been worn a few times and the laundress has done her worst with them, they go a bad colour and get stretched.

A good collar will last longer and look better than a cheap collar but it goes before the laundress's iron in time.

The man who would be well dressed always buys the same kind of shirt, and precisely the same size of collars.

If you pick up a good collar and lay it flat down on the table, you will see that it is not merely a straight strip of linen; it is shaped in such a way that when buttoned it fits on to the neck of the shirt closely.

The original glossy beauty of a collar can quickly be lost as the wearer becomes hot. It is, however, quite easy for a man to bring an extra collar in the pocket of his overcoat.

A narrow width is the best collar that a man can possibly buy when he is going to play golf, or ride a bicycle, or take any hard exercise.

Collars should be kept in special round collar-boxes; ties should be folded neatly when taken off, and put away in a tie-case.

If the collar fits properly, the tie ought not to be very unruly.

Dress ties may be of fine pique or plain muslin or fine cambric with a tiny indistinct check (of course in white). As a rule the dress ties that you buy are too long. A bow tie - dress or otherwise - should not be longer than about 32 inches.

A greasy necktie is an unpardonable sin.

*When you have once tied a bow properly
the matter becomes easier and easier
at every attempt.*

✑ A Useful Hint ✑

The following method is the simplest way to
tie a bow tie.

Put the tie round your neck with the left-hand
end about a couple of inches below the right.

Tie in a single knot and bring the left-hand
end - which should still be the longer of the two
- over so that it covers the right.

Make the left-hand loop of the bow with the
right-hand end, which should then be at right
angles to the left.

Then bring the left hand end up so that it goes
right round the left-hand loop.

Then fold the left-hand end and push it
through the centre loop which has been formed.

If this is done properly the left-hand end
makes the right-hand bow of the tie, and all that
remains to be done is to pull the under part of the
two bows tightly and the tie will be fixed.

CUFF LINKS AND ORNAMENTS

... more manly and aristocratic ...

It is not considered good taste for a man to wear much jewellery. A plain handsome ring, studs and sleeve-links, a watch-chain without pendants, will always look more manly and aristocratic than a great display of elaborate ornaments.

At Christmas time the jewellers' shop windows blossom out into all sorts of pretty things, among them being variegated studs and links. Whatever links a man puts into his cuffs, he must absolutely refrain from putting any but the plainest of studs into his shirt front.

Coloured cuff links should never be worn when in mourning.

As a general rule,
the less jewellery a man wears the better.

GLOVES

indispensably necessary ...

Gloves should be nice, but not too nice.

A dark tan glove always looks well in a man's hand, but there is too much of a suggestion of a linendraper's shopman about spotless lavender kids.

A gentleman should always wear gloves when in town, particularly when paying calls, in the street, at the opera or the play, but not at dinner.

Gloves are indispensably necessary in a ballroom; it would be quite as correct for a gentleman to be seen dancing without his coat as without his gloves.

When taking refreshment, pull them off;
it is vulgar to eat in gloves.

⁀ℰ *A Useful Hint* ℰ⁀

Choose gloves too large rather than too small.
A man's hand looks foolish squeezed into
a tight glove.

HATS

The well–dressed man doesn't follow fashions slavishly ...

The fashion in hats changes rather rapidly and it is as well to remember that the well-dressed man doesn't follow the fashions slavishly, but only those that are becoming to him.

Some men have their hats ventilated by having a hole punched in the centre of the crown. One hole is not enough; there should be at least one more in the side of the crown, if the hat is to be properly ventilated.

The straw hat scarcely varies in shape from year to year. To derive the maximum comfort from the wearing of a straw hat, don't have any lining in the crown and have a strip of flannel instead of leather round the part of the crown that touches the head.

*The well-dressed man
knows that finishing touches can impart
a gentlemanly tone to the appearance.*

BOOTS AND SHOES

Boots should be well vaselined ...

However low you sink in the world you should never get quite so low that you lose the desire to have clean boots.

Boots and shoes should not be allowed to litter a man's dressing-room.

Brown boots may be worn in the country all the year round. They are much cooler than black boots. Most men fight shy of putting on new brown boots the first time, because they always look so aggressively new.

A good way to tone down the bright shade of tan is to wash the boots with a little saddle soap. Dry them well before you put them on. This will darken them slightly and every time they are cleaned, the darkening process will be repeated.

Have button boots to wear in town and lace boots to wear in the country. If you must wear shoes in town in the summer - they are not so becoming as boots and make the feet appear larger then they really are - have them made to fit you.

A good pair of boots look better
when they are nearly worn out than
a cheap pair when they are new.

A small trunk or suit-case stand usually forms part of every dressing-room's equipment. The suit-case is placed on the top of this, and the boots neatly ranged on the shelf underneath. All the boots should be placed on trees when not in wear.

If put away for any length of time, boots should be well vaselined to prevent the leather from cracking.

There are men for whom patent boots are comfortable, even on the hottest day. Patent boots are really the most unsatisfactory of all boots. You can never be sure that a new pair won't crack the first time you wear them.

๛ *A Useful Hint* ๛

Warm a new pair of patents before the fire before you put them on, and at the same time rub them slightly with a soft cloth. The friction and the warmth make the leather pliable, and then the boots probably won't crack.

EVENING DRESS FOR GENTLEMEN

A flower ... one of the few allowable devices to brighten up his attire ...

When a gentleman is invited out for the evening he need not be embarrassed as to what he shall wear. He has not to consider whether he shall wear blue or pink, or whether the Joneses will notice if he wears the same attire three times running.

Fashion has ordained that he shall always wear a black dress suit in the evening, with only a white waistcoat as an occasional relief. His necktie must be white, his gloves white or light-coloured.

An excess of jewellery is to be avoided in the evening, but he may wear gold or diamond studs, and a watch-chain. He may also wear a flower in his button-hole, for this is one of the few allowable devices by which he may brighten up his attire.

Plain and simple as the dress is, it is a sure test of a gentlemanly appearance. The man who dines in evening dress every night of his life looks easy and natural in it, whereas the man who takes to it late in life generally succeeds in looking like a waiter.

IN THE COUNTRY

Some country people are old-fashioned ...

When you put on a tweed suit you should be in the country and you need not be so particular about your clothes as when you are in town.

However, even if you are wearing a tweed suit there is no necessity for you to have baggy trousers!

Many men are bothered to know what to wear on Sundays in the country. Some country people are strictly old-fashioned in this matter, and expect their guests to put on town clothes on a Sunday morning. Other hosts are quite content if you wear a black lounge jacket and waistcoat and grey trousers – or even a navy blue serge lounge suit.

If you are in any doubt, take your town clothes with you.

Don't wear thin button boots with a knicker-bocker suit. Wear shoes or stout walking boots.

In the country, a high hat looks ridiculous, and would only be worn by a snob!

ᴗ *A Useful Hint* ᴗ

When you are ordering a tweed suit order two
pairs of trousers to each coat and waistcoat. A
coat and waistcoat will always last two pairs of
trousers. In this way you can wear the trousers on
alternate occasions - and if you take three such
suits with you into the country you can always be
sure of having your trousers in good order.

TRAVELLING

... a full view of your boots ...

If you are travelling a good deal, have a proper travelling suit of grey worsted material. Worsted does not easily stretch or get out of shape or go into creases.

Wear gloves when you are travelling, even though the weather be warm. Gloves keep the hands clean, and if they are of thin suede they are not warm.

A careful man is always extra particular about his boots when he is travelling. You cannot very well be in a railway carriage without allowing your fellow-passengers to have a full view of your boots.

When cycling, if you can, always wear gaiter trousers. These are like a pair of trousers altered so that they were not at all full over the thighs and knees and fitted closely to the calf, tapering towards the feet and ending in a pair of spats made out of the same trouser material.

They are used by gentlemen who have to cycle but who cannot appear in knickerbockers. Doctors and clergymen find these gaiter trousers very useful. If you ride in ordinary trousers and fasten with clips, you spoil the trousers and pull them out of shape.

When motoring, special garments will be necessary in order to drive in any comfort in an open automobile.

The wind will pass through tweed overcoats, and the first requirement is that the clothes should be air-proof and be so contrived as to prevent the wind from getting under them,

A leather jacket and leather trousers are objectionable because moisture from the body cannot escape. Leather may, however, be used as a lining to cloth clothes provided that it is bored with many small holes through which the moisture from the body may evaporate.

If the automobilist does not use a thick rug to protect his legs, gaiters should be worn with knickerbockers and, if trousers are worn, they should be bound tightly round the ankles when driving.

As regards underclothing, silk is perhaps the best material for retaining the warmth of the body.

∾ *A Useful Hint* ∾

The proper way to fold a coat when travelling:
Stretch it out lining downwards on a big table
(use the bed if necessary). Turn the collar of the
coat up. Pull out the sleeves well and flatten them
with your hands so that the seams come to the
extreme edges. If you are folding a lounge coat
fold back the two sides of the coat over the
sleeves, double the coat in half, and there you are.
If you are folding a dress coat or morning coat
turn up the tails as far as they will go before you
double the coat up.

*If you are not getting ahead as
quickly as you would like, try the moral
effect of a new suit.*

THRIFT

Purchase nothing not absolutely needful ...

A personal scheme of dress expenditure mainly consists of self-control and thrift. These qualities cannot be valued too highly.

Never spend a shilling when sixpence will suffice, never purchase anything not absolutely needful, waste nothing, and economise on clothes by taking due care of them.

Keep a strict account of your dress expenditure, and be very apt in comparing one year's outlay with another, so as to learn the lessons of each year's demands and experiences.

A fixed time for a thorough review of the wardrobe is also needful; and likewise a fixed period for the renewal of certain expensive articles.

THE RIGHT CLOTHES FOR THE RIGHT OCCASION

Clothes at a wedding

If the wedding is in the summer, the best get-up consists of a grey frock-coat, silk hat, grey suede gloves, patent or glace kid boots, light waistcoat and rather dark grey tie.

It is a mistake to wear a light tie with a light waistcoat. If you are wearing a waistcoat of the same material as the coat, then you can wear a white tie – of plain soft silk – or a light grey tie.

If the wedding is in the winter, you would wear a black frock coat and waistcoat, grey striped trousers, glace kid or patent boots and grey suede or buckskin gloves.

Lavender-coloured trousers to wear at weddings have gone out of fashion.

A Function in Town

The same clothes would do equally well at any big function in town, and in summer you would wear the summer frock-coat suit at a garden-party in town.

A well-dressed man will wear similar clothes at most race meetings, but in the last few years the Prince of Wales has led the fashion at Goodwood by putting on a lounge suit and straw hat instead of a frock-coat suit and silk hat. His Royal Highness always goes to the Derby in a frock-coat suit - possibly because Derby Day is seldom so hot as the first day at Goodwood. At Ascot most men wear frock or morning coat suits.

GOOD ADVICE

In town.

When you are in town you mustn't appear in a lounge suit and a bowler after lunch and of course if you had any business appointment in the morning, you would wear a frock or morning coat suit and silk hat.

The summer months.

You may make an exception to these rules in the summer. In August and September society people are not supposed to be in town, and therefore if you happen to be in town you can wear country clothes – a light thin lounge suit and a straw hat. If you are in town in August or September, you are supposed to be there only because you are passing through on your way to the country!

Boots.

Don't wear tan boots or shoes with a black coat. Tan boots are intended to be worn in the country and black coats in town; the two do not go well together.

GOOD ADVICE

Your bed as a trouser press.

A very good plan is to place the trousers so folded under the mattress of a bed, as the pressure thus afforded answers the same purpose as that of trouser-stretchers, and helps to prevent them from becoming baggy at the knees.

Underwear.

Cheap underwear is even a greater mistake with men than with women.

Darn your new socks.

It is a wise plan to stretch the heels and toes of new socks and have them lightly darned before use; they will be found to wear much longer in this way.

Servants.

Cleanliness of person and propriety of dress are worthy the attention of all persons. Neatness and respectability of appearance should always be expected of servants, whether they have high or low wages.

ACKNOWLEDGEMENTS

The compiler and publishers would like to thank the following:

Burberrys
Alfred Dunhill Limited
Taylors of Bond Street
Other pictures from private collections

THE ETIQUETTE COLLECTION
Collect the set!

THE ETIQUETTE OF AN ENGLISH TEA
THE ETIQUETTE OF ENGLISH PUDDINGS
ETIQUETTE FOR COFFEE LOVERS
ETIQUETTE FOR CHOCOLATE LOVERS

THE ETIQUETTE OF MOTORING
ETIQUETTE FOR THE CHAUFFEUR

ETIQUETTE FOR GENTLEMEN
THE ETIQUETTE OF POLITENESS
THE ETIQUETTE OF DRESS
THE ETIQUETTE OF LOVE AND COURTSHIP
THE ETIQUETTE OF NAMING THE BABY

A Copper Beech Book makes the perfect gift. See also our books about parlour games, servants, graphology and social secrets.

For your free catalogue containing these and other Copper Beech Gift Books, write to:

Copper Beech Publishing Ltd
P O Box 159 East Grinstead Sussex England RH19 4FS

*Copper Beech Gift Books
are designed and printed
in Great Britain.*